EXPLORE

THE
MEANING
OF

Published in North America by Alpha North America, 2275 Half Day Road
Suite 185, Deerfield, IL 60015

© 1993 Alpha International, Holy Trinity Brompton, Brompton Road, London
SW7 1JA, UK

The Alpha Course Manual

This edition first printed by Alpha North America in 2008

Printed in the United States of America

Scripture in this publication is from the Holy Bible, New International Version
(NIV), Copyright 1973, 1978, 1984 International Bible Society, used by permission
of Zondervan. All rights reserved.

ISBN 978-1-934564-58-5

1 2 3 4 5 6 7 8 9 10 Printing/Year 12 11 10 09 08

CONTENTS

IS THERE MORE TO LIFE

Welcome to the Alpha course—an opportunity to explore the meaning of life

Over 11 million people worldwide, from every walk of life, have already been on an Alpha course.

This manual outlines the content of the 15 talks, which each look at a different aspect of the Christian faith. After each talk, there is a time for discussion in small groups—a place where you can ask questions, delve into different issues, find out what others think, and perhaps make some new friends along the way!

INTRODUCTION

- Objections
- Misconceptions
- What does Christianity have to do with life today?

1. DIRECTION FOR A LOST WORLD

- Hunger for meaning and purpose
- Questions to ask about life:
  - what am I doing on earth?
  - what is the point of life?
  - where am I heading?

Jesus: "I AM THE WAY"

2. REALITY IN A CONFUSED WORLD

Does it matter what we believe?

- Truth—understood intellectually
- Truth—experienced as a relationship

Jesus: "I AM THE TRUTH"

3. LIFE IN A DARK WORLD

- Created in God's image
- Fallen into sin
- Forgiven in Christ

Jesus: "I AM THE LIFE"

JESUS SAID, "I AM THE WAY, THE TRUTH AND THE LIFE" [JOHN 14:6]

CONCLUSION

- Not boring; it is about living life to the full
- Not untrue; it is the truth
- Not irrelevant; it transforms the whole of our lives

Recommended reading

Why Jesus?
Nicky Gumbel
Alpha North America
20072

Why Christmas?
Nicky Gumbel
Alpha North America
20081

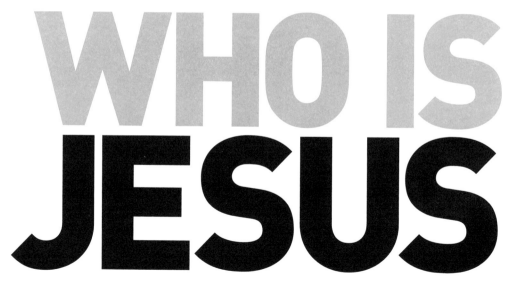

WHO IS
JESUS

INTRODUCTION

1. He existed

- Evidence outside the New Testament about Jesus includes:
  - Tacitus & Suetonius, Roman historians
  - Josephus, Jewish historian

- Evidence within the New Testament:
  - F. F. Bruce

WAS HE MORE THAN JUST:

a man : a great human : a religious teacher?

(Matthew 16:13 –16)

2. He was fully human

- Human body
  - tired (John 4:6)
  - hungry (Matthew 4:2)

- Human emotions
  - anger (Mark 11:15–17)
  - love (Mark 10:21)
  - sadness (John 11:32–36)

- Human experiences
  - temptation (Mark 1:13)
  - learning (Luke 2:46–52)
  - work (Mark 6:3)
  - obedience (Luke 2:51)

ISSUE: HOW DO WE KNOW THAT WHAT THEY
WROTE DOWN HAS NOT BEEN CHANGED OVER THE YEARS?

WORK	WHEN WRITTEN	EARLIEST COPY	TIME LAPSE	COPIES
Herodotus	488-428 B.C.	A.D. 900	1,300 years	8
Thucydides	c.460-400 B.C.	c. A.D. 900	1,300 years	8
Tacitus	A.D. 100	A.D. 1100	1,000 years	20
Caesar's Gallic War	58-50 B.C.	A.D. 900	950 years	9-10
Livy's Roman History	59 B.C.-A.D. 17	A.D. 900	900 years	20
New Testament	A.D. 40-100	A.D. 130 (full manuscripts A.D. 350)	300 years	5,000 + (Greek) 10,000 (Latin) 9,300 (Other)

1. WHAT DID HE SAY ABOUT HIMSELF?

1. Teaching centered on Himself

- I am
  - "I am the bread of life" (John 6:35)
  - "I am the light of the world" (John 8:12)
  - "I am the resurrection and the life" (John 11:25, 26)
  - "I am the way and the truth and the life" (John 14:6)
- "My kingdom" (Luke 22:30)
- "Come to me" (Matthew 11:28, 29)
- "Follow me" (Mark 1:17)
- Receive me—receive God (Matthew 10:40)
- Welcome me—welcome God (Mark 9:37)
- To have seen me is to have seen God (John 14:9)
- Claims humanity's supreme love (Matthew 10:37; Luke 14:26)

2. His indirect claims

- To forgive sins (Mark 2:5)
- To judge the world (Matthew 25:31, 32, 40, 45)

3. His direct claims

- Messiah (Mark 14:61, 62)
- Son of God (Mark 14:61)
- God the Son
  - ". . . before Abraham was born, I am!" (John 8:58)
  - "my Lord and my God" (John 20:26–29)
  - "claim to be God" (John 10:30–33)

C. S. LEWIS WROTE:

"A MAN WHO WAS MERELY A MAN AND SAID THE SORT OF THINGS JESUS SAID WOULD NOT BE A GREAT MORAL TEACHER."

He would either be insane or else he would be "the Devil of Hell." "You must make your choice," he writes. Either Jesus was, and is, the Son of God or else He was insane or evil but, C. S. Lewis goes on, "Let us not come up with any patronizing nonsense about his being a great human teacher. He has not left that open to us. He did not intend to."

"We are faced then with a frightening alternative." Either Jesus was (and is) exactly what He said or else He was insane or something worse. To C. S. Lewis it seemed clear that He could neither have been insane or evil and thus he concludes, "However strange or terrifying or unlikely it may seem, I have to accept the view that He was and is God."

2. WHAT EVIDENCE IS THERE TO SUPPORT WHAT HE SAID?

- His teaching
  - i.e., Sermon on the Mount (Matthew 5–7)
- His works (John 10:37, 38)
- His character
- His fulfilment of Old Testament prophecy
- His conquest of death

EVIDENCE FOR THE RESURRECTION:

1. His absence from the tomb

- Theories:
  - Jesus did not die (John 19:33–34)
  - disciples stole the body
  - authorities stole the body
  - robbers stole the body (John 20:1–9)

2. His presence with the disciples

- Hallucination?
- Number of appearances
  - at least eleven different occasions
  - 500+ people
  - period of six weeks
- Nature of appearances (Luke 24:36–43)

3. Immediate effect

- Birth and growth of Christian church

4. Effect down the ages

- Experience of Christians down the ages

CONCLUSION

- There is a lot of evidence to support Jesus' existence
- Christians believe He is the Son of God

Recommended reading
Alpha—Questions of Life
Nicky Gumbel
Alpha North America
105022

INTRODUCTION

THE CROSS LIES AT THE HEART OF THE CHRISTIAN FAITH (1 Corinthians 2:2)

1. THE PROBLEM

"All have sinned . . ." (Romans 3:23)

- Results of sin:
  - pollution of sin (Mark 7:20–23)
  - power of sin (John 8:34)
  - penalty for sin (Romans 6:23)
  - partition of sin (Isaiah 59:2)

2. THE SOLUTION

- "The self-substitution of God" – John Stott (1 Peter 2:24)
- Agony of the cross (Isaiah 53:6)

3. THE RESULT (Romans 3:21–26)

Four images:

1. The Temple
- "God presented him as a sacrifice of atonement, through faith in his blood" (v.25)
- (Hebrews 10:4)
- (1 John 1:7)
- Pollution of sin removed

2. The Market Place
- "The redemption that came by Christ Jesus" (v.24)
- Power of sin broken (John 8:36)

3. The Law Court
- "Justified freely by his grace" (v.24)
- Penalty of sin paid

4. The Home
- Reconciliation

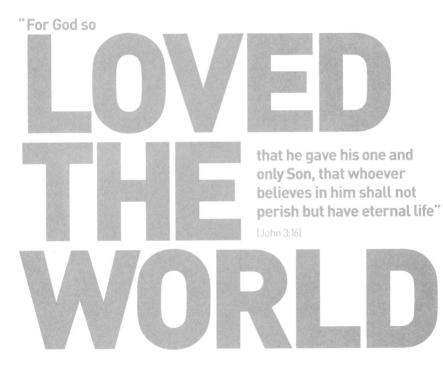

"For God so LOVED THE WORLD that he gave his one and only Son, that whoever believes in him shall not perish but have eternal life"

(John 3:16)

- "God was . . . in Christ"
  (2 Corinthians 5:19)
- Partition of sin destroyed

CONCLUSION

- "Righteousness from God"
  (Romans 3:22; Isaiah 53:6)
- He died for you and me
  (Galatians 2:20)

Recommended reading
Mere Christianity
C. S. Lewis
Zondervan
ISBN 97800060652920

Basic Christianity
John Stott
IVP
ISBN 9780830834037

Orthodoxy
G. K. Chesterton
Hendrickson
ISBN 9781598560572

HOW CAN WE

INTRODUCTION

". . . those who become Christians
become new persons. They are not
the same anymore, for the old is gone.
A new life has begun!"
(2 Corinthians 5:17, New Living Translation)

But experiences vary . . . some
immediately know the difference . . .
for others it is more gradual

- **When we received Christ, we
  became a child of God** (John 1:12)
  (Note: believed + received)
- **God wants us to be sure**
  – "I write these things to you who believe
    in the name of the Son of God so that
    you may know that you have eternal life"
    (1 John 5:13)

1. THE WORD OF GOD

We must not only trust our feelings,
which can be changeable and may
even be deceptive at times, but instead
rely on God's promises

- "I will come in" (Revelation 3:20)
- "I am with you always" (Matthew 28:20)
- "I give them eternal life" (John 10:28)

Faith = taking God's promises and
daring to believe them

2. THE WORK OF JESUS

We cannot earn God's forgiveness, but Jesus Christ died on the cross so that we might be reconciled to God

- Gift of God (Romans 6:23)
- God loves us and died to prove it (John 3:16)
- He took our sins upon Himself (Isaiah 53:6; 2 Corinthians 5:21)

3. THE WITNESS OF THE SPIRIT

When someone becomes a Christian, God's Holy Spirit comes to live inside them (Romans 8:9)

1. He transforms us from within

- Our characters (Galatians 5:22, 23)
- Our relationships

Which of the following changes have you already experienced in your life?

- new love for God
- desire to read the Bible
- sense of forgiveness
- new concern for others
- enjoyment of worshiping God
- desire to meet with other Christians

2. He brings a deep, personal conviction that I am God's child

- (Romans 8:15, 16)

CONCLUSION

- Make a decision to take a step of faith by inviting Jesus in
  - It is not irrational
  - It is a step of faith based on evidence
  - The Holy Spirit testifies to our spirit that we are children of God and that we're loved by Him (Romans 8:15, 16)

Recommended reading

Run Baby Run
Nicky Cruz
Bridge-Logos
ISBN 9780882706306

The Cross & the Switchblade
David Wilkerson
Baker Publishing
ISBN 9780800794460

The Hiding Place
Corrie Ten Boom
Baker Publishing
ISBN 9780800794057

WHY AND HOW DO I...

INTRODUCTION

- Prayer is as important for Christians as communication is to any relationship; it helps us develop a relationship with God. Prayer is a two-way conversation with Him—He hears our prayers and we can learn to listen to what He may have to say in response

- Praying can give Christians peace and help them to experience God's love—these are just some of the rewards of prayer

- Prayer allows Christians to have access to God through Jesus, His Son

1. WHAT IS CHRISTIAN PRAYER? (Matthew 6:5–13)

- The most important activity of our lives (Ephesians 2:18)
- The whole Trinity involved

1. To the Father (Matthew 6)
- "To your father" (v.6)
  - immanence
- "In heaven" (v.9)
  - transcendence (Matthew 6)

2. Through the Son
- (Ephesians 2:18)

3. By the Spirit
- (Romans 8:26)

2. WHY PRAY? (Matthew 6:6)

1. Model of Jesus (Mark 1:35)

- "When you pray"
  (Luke 6:12, 9:18, 28, 11:1)

2. Developing a relationship with God, for which we are created

3. Rewards of prayer (Matthew 6:6)

- Joy (John 16:24)
- Peace (Philippians 4:6, 7)

4. Results of prayer (Matthew 7:7–11)

3. DOES GOD ALWAYS ANSWER PRAYER? (Matthew 7:7–11)

Our prayers may not be answered if there is:

- Unconfessed sin (Isaiah 59:2)
- Unforgiveness (Matthew 6:14, 15)
- Disobedience (1 John 3:21, 22)
- Wrong motives (James 4:2, 3)
- Misunderstanding of the will of God
  - "good gifts" (Matthew 7:11)
- Yes/no/wait
  - no:
    "either not good in themselves, or not good for us or for others, directly or indirectly, immediately or ultimately"
    John Stott

4. HOW DO WE PRAY?

A: adoration
C: confession
T: thanksgiving
S: supplication (requests)

Model of the Lord's Prayer
(Matthew 6:9–13)

- "Our Father in heaven" (v.9)
- "Hallowed be your name" (v.9)
- "Your kingdom come" (v.10)
  - God's rule and reign in people's lives
  - return of Jesus
  - presence of God's kingdom now
- "Your will be done on earth
  as it is in heaven" (v.10)
- "Give us today our daily bread" (v.11)

"Everything necessary for the preservation of life, like food, a healthy body, good weather, house, home, wife, children, good government and peace"
Martin Luther

- "Forgive us our debts as we also have forgiven our debtors" (v.12)
- "Lead us not into temptation but deliver us from the evil one" (v.13)

5. WHEN SHOULD WE PRAY?

1. Always
- (1 Thessalonians 5:17)
- (Ephesians 6:18)

2. Alone (Matthew 6:6)
- Regular pattern
- Best part of the day (Mark 1:35)

3. With others
- (Matthew 18:19)

CONCLUSION

- Prayer is part of a relationship with God
  - pray to develop this relationship
  - be honest in prayer
- Pray always:
  - ACTS
- Pray alone and with others

Recommended reading

Too Busy Not to Pray
Bill Hybels
IVP
ISBN 9780851113296

The Power of Simple Prayer
Joyce Meyer
Faithwords
ISBN 9780446531962

Prayer
Philip Yancey
Zondervan
ISBN 9780310271055

WHY
HOW
I
THE

AND
SHOULD
READ
BIBLE?

INTRODUCTION

- The most popular book
- The most powerful book
- The most precious book

(Matthew 4:4)

1. GOD HAS SPOKEN: REVELATION

- Inspired by God
- Difficulties in the Bible
  - historical difficulties (cf. Luke 3:1–2)
  - moral difficulties (i.e., issue of suffering)
- (2 Timothy 3:16–17)
- "Theopneustos"—God-breathed

Therefore it is our authority for:

- Teaching
- Rebuking
- Correcting
- Training in righteousness
  - i.e., our manual for life

2. GOD SPEAKS: RELATIONSHIP

"Salvation through faith in Christ"
(2 Timothy 3:15; John 5:39, 40)

1. To those who are not Christians
(Romans 10:17; John 20:31)

2. To those who are Christians

- Become like Jesus (2 Corinthians 3:18)
- Joy and peace in the midst of a storm (Psalm 23:5)
- Guidance (Psalm 119:105)
- Health/healing (Proverbs 4:20–22)
- Defense against spiritual attack (Matthew 4:1–11)
- Power (Hebrews 4:12)
- Cleansing (John 15:3)

3. HOW DO WE HEAR GOD SPEAK THROUGH THE BIBLE?

1. Time
- Plan ahead
- Develop a regular pattern

2. Place
- "A solitary place" (Mark 1:35)

3. Method
- Ask God to speak
- Read the passage
  (try using Bible reading notes)
- Ask yourself:
  – what does it say?
  – what does it mean?
  – how does it apply?
- Respond in prayer
- Put it into practice
  – "everyone who hears these words of mine and puts them into practice . . ." (Matthew 7:24)

CONCLUSION

- God speaks to us through the Bible
- Make a habit of reading the Bible regularly

Recommended reading

Holy Bible, New International Version (New International Version is used in the DVDs, but we recommend any modern version)

How to Read the Bible for All Its Worth Gordon Fee & Douglas Stuart Zondervan ISBN 9780310246046

The New Lion Handbook to the Bible Lion ISBN 9780745938707

30 Days Nicky Gumbel Alpha International Publications 54057

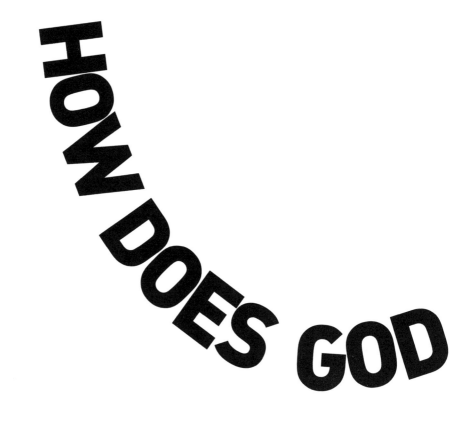

INTRODUCTION

- Decisions, i.e.: marriage, job, home, money, giving, holidays, use of time, possessions, etc.

1. God promises to guide

- (Psalm 32:8)
- (John 10:3, 4, 27)

2. God has a good plan for our lives

- (Jeremiah 29:11)
- (Romans 12:2)
- (John 10:10, 15)

3. We need to consult God before making major decisions

- (Isaiah 30:1, 2)
- Jesus is the supreme example
  - (Luke 4:1)
  - (John 5:19)

4. Our attitude needs to be one of humility

- (Psalm 25:9, 14)
- "I am the Lord's servant and I am willing to do whatever he wants" (Luke 1:38, Living Bible)

1. COMMANDING SCRIPTURE

1. General will (2 Timothy 3:16)

- General instruction for marriage, work, money, children, elderly relatives

2. Particular will

- (Psalm 119:105, 130–133) May bring to light a particular verse

2. COMPELLING SPIRIT (Acts 20:22)

"They know his voice" (John 10:3, 4; Acts 16:7)

1. God speaks as you pray (Acts 13:1–3)

- The good thought
- Strong impressions
- Feelings

2. Strong desire to do something

- "To will and to act according to his good purpose" (Philippians 2:13)

3. Sometimes He guides in more unusual ways

- Prophecy, i.e., Agabus (Acts 11:27, 28; 21:10, 11)
- Dreams (Matthew 1:20)
- Visions/pictures (Acts 16:10)
- Angels (Genesis 18; Matthew 2:19; Acts 12:7)
- Audible voice (1 Samuel 3:4–14)

4. Need for testing (1 John 4:1)

- Is it loving? (1 John 4:16)
- Is it in line with the Bible?
- Is it strengthening, encouraging, and comforting? (1 Corinthians 14:3)
- Does it bring the peace of God? (Colossians 3:15)

3. COMMON SENSE

"Do not be like the horse or the mule, which have no understanding but must be controlled by bit and bridle" (Psalm 32:8, 9)

- "Reflect on what I am saying, for the Lord will give you insight into all this" (2 Timothy 2:7)
- "God's promises of guidance were not given to save us the problem of thinking" John Stott
  – i.e., marriage, job/career
    (1 Corinthians 7:17–24)

4. COUNSEL OF SAINTS

- ". . . the wise listen to advice" (Proverbs 12:15)
- "Plans fail for lack of counsel, but with many advisers they succeed" (Proverbs 15:22)
- "Make plans by seeking advice" (Proverbs 20:18)

But:
- Who is responsible?
- Whom should we consult?

"AND SO AFTER WAITING PATIENTLY, ABRAHAM RECEIVED WHAT WAS PROMISED" (Hebrews 6:15)

5. CIRCUMSTANTIAL SIGNS

- "In your heart you plan your course, but the Lord determines your steps" (Proverbs 16:9; Psalm 37:5)

- Sometimes God closes doors (Acts 16:7)

- Sometimes God opens doors (1 Corinthians 16:9)

- Watch the circumstances but don't put too much weight on them

- Sometimes we need to persevere despite the circumstances

CONCLUSION

- Be patient

- We all make mistakes—God forgives (Joel 2:25)

- (Romans 8:28)

Recommended reading

The Joy of Listening to God
Joyce Huggett
IVP
ISBN 9780877847298

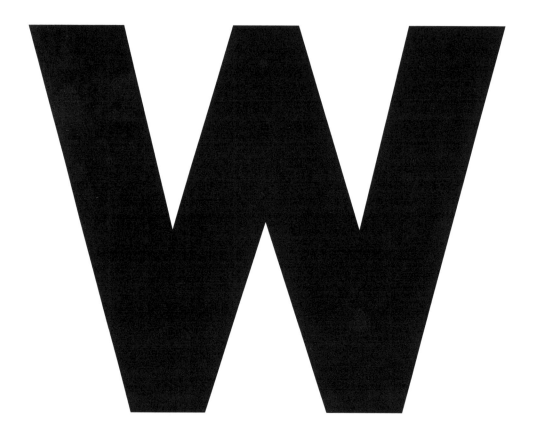

IS THE HOLY SPIRIT?

INTRODUCTION

For a long time in the church the person and work of the Holy Spirit has been:

- Ignored
  - a greater concentration on the Father and the Son
- Misunderstood
  - "Holy Ghost," "He" not "it," resisted
  - He wants to take control

1. HE WAS INVOLVED IN CREATION

- Bringing order out of chaos (Genesis 1:1–2)
- Giving life to man (Genesis 2:7)

2. HE CAME UPON PARTICULAR PEOPLE AT PARTICULAR TIMES FOR PARTICULAR TASKS

- Gideon—for leadership (Judges 6:14–16)
- Samson—for strength (Judges 15:14, 15)
- Bezalel—for artistic work (Exodus 31:1–5)
- Isaiah—for prophecy (Isaiah 61:1–3)

3. HE WAS PROMISED BY THE FATHER

- The promise of a "new thing"
  - ". . . they will all know me"
    (Jeremiah 31:31–34)
  - "I will put my Spirit in you"
    (Ezekiel 36:26, 27)
  - "a river flowing from the Temple"
    (Ezekiel 47)
  - "I will pour out my Spirit on all people"
    (Joel 2:28, 29)

However, the prophecies remained unfulfilled for at least 300 years

With the coming of Jesus there is a great activity of the Spirit

- But still on a few particular people:
  - John the Baptist (Luke 1:15)
  - Mary (Luke 1:35)
  - Elizabeth (Luke 1:41)
  - Zechariah (Luke 1:67)
  - Simeon (Luke 2:25–27)

4. JOHN THE BAPTIST LINKS HIM WITH JESUS (Luke 3:16)

In Greek "baptizdo" = to overwhelm, immerse, plunge, drench

- Jesus, the Spirit-filled man
  - Jesus received power through the anointing of the Holy Spirit at His baptism (Luke 3:22; Luke 4:1, 14, 18)

5. JESUS PREDICTS HIS PRESENCE (John 7:37–38)

However, He tells them to wait in the city until they are clothed with power from on high (Luke 24:49; Acts 1:4, 5, 8; Acts 2:2–4)

- At Pentecost the disciples were filled with the Spirit and received:
  - new languages (Acts 2:4–12)
  - new boldness (Acts 2:14)
  - new power (Acts 2:37–41)

"When the people heard this, they were cut to the heart and said to Peter and the other apostles, 'Brothers, what shall we do?' . . . and about

3000

were added to their number that day" (Acts 2:37, 41)

CONCLUSION

- We live in the age of the Spirit. God has promised to give His Spirit to every Christian
  (Acts 2:37–39)

Recommended reading

Chasing the Dragon
Jackie Pullinger
Regal Books
ISBN 9789830743827

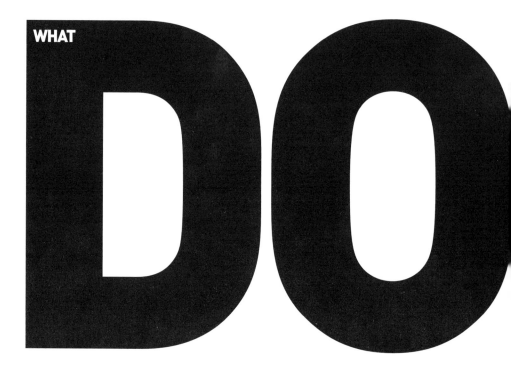

WHAT

DO

ES

THE HOLY SPIRIT DO?

INTRODUCTION

- New birth (John 3:3–8)
- Born into a family

1. SONS AND DAUGHTERS OF GOD

1. Forgiveness (Romans 8:1, 2)

2. Adoption (Romans 8:14–17)
- Greatest privilege (v.14)
- Closest intimacy (v.15)
- Deepest experience (v.16)
- Greatest security (v.17)

2. DEVELOPING THE RELATIONSHIP (Ephesians 2:18)

1. He helps us to pray (Romans 8:26)

2. He enables us to understand God's word (Ephesians 1:17, 18)

3. THE FAMILY LIKENESS

- (2 Corinthians 3:18)
- (Galatians 5:22, 23)

4. UNITY IN THE FAMILY

- (Ephesians 4:3–6)

5. GIFTS FOR ALL THE CHILDREN

Each member of the family is different (1 Corinthians 12:4–11)

- Free gifts
- To each one
- For the common good

6. THE GROWING FAMILY

- He empowers us to be witnesses for Christ
- Power for service (Acts 1:8)

CONCLUSION

- Every Christian has the Holy Spirit (Romans 8:9) but not every Christian is filled with the Spirit
  - "be filled" (Ephesians 5:18–20)
  - how? (Revelation 22:17)

Recommended reading

The God Who Changes Lives 1, 2, 3 & 4
Ed. M. Elsdon-Dew
Alpha International Publications
Vol. 1 ISBN 9781902750774
Vol. 2 ISBN 9781902750781
Vol. 3 ISBN 9781902750620
Vol. 4 ISBN 9781904074564
The American Collection 100651

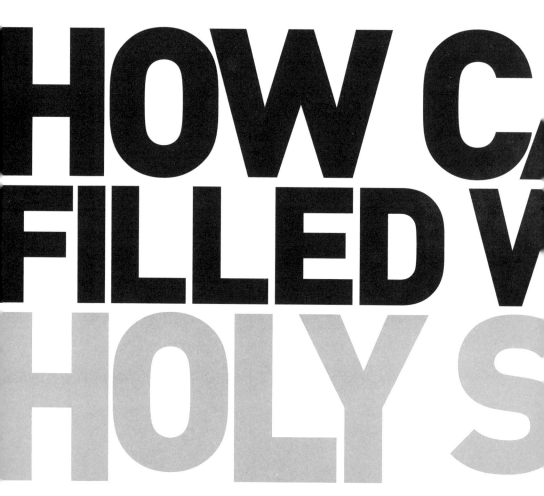

INTRODUCTION

Outpouring of the Spirit in Acts:

5 Categories:

1. Longing (Pentecost – Acts 2:2–4)

2. Receptive (Samaria – Acts 8:14–23)

3. Hostile (Paul – Acts 8:1, 3; 9:1–2)

4. Uninformed (Ephesus - Acts 19:1–6)

5. Unlikely (Gentiles - Acts 10:44–47)

What happened to Cornelius and his household when the Spirit came upon them? (Acts 10:44–46)

1. THEY EXPERIENCED THE POWER OF THE HOLY SPIRIT

". . . the Holy Spirit came on all who heard the message. The circumcised believers. . . were astonished" (Acts 10:44, 45)

- Experience is different for everyone
  - (Acts 8:16)
  - (Romans 5:5)
  - (Ephesians 3:14–19)
- Fruit of the Spirit

2. THEY WERE RELEASED IN PRAISE

"For they heard them . . . praising God" (Acts 10:46)

- Fear of emotion
- All relationships should involve emotions
- Private versus public
- Emotion versus emotionalism

3. THEY RECEIVED A NEW LANGUAGE

"For they heard them speaking in tongues" (Acts 10:46)

1. Not all Christians speak in tongues

- Not necessarily a sign of being filled with the Spirit
- There are no first or second-class Christians
- It is not the most important gift

2. What is the gift of tongues?

- Human or angelic language (1 Corinthians 13:1)
- A form of prayer (1 Corinthians 14:2)
- Builds up individual
- Transcends language barrier (1 Corinthians 14:14)
- Speaker in full control

3. Why is it helpful?
- Praise/worship
- Praying for oneself
- Praying for others

4. Does the New Testament approve?
(1 Corinthians 14)
- Context: excessive public use
- Nevertheless . . . (vv.5, 18, 39)
- Private versus public

5. How do we receive this gift?
- "Eagerly desire" (1 Corinthians 14:1)
- Ask God
- Co-operate with the Spirit
- Believe
- Persevere

CONCLUSION

Three common hindrances
(Luke 11:9–13)

1. Doubt (vv.9, 10)

2. Fear (vv.11–13)

3. Inadequacy (v.13)

Recommended reading
Paul, the Spirit and the People of God
Gordon D. Fee
Hendrickson
ISBN 9781565631700

The Mystery of Pentecost
Raniero Cantalamessa
Liturgical Press
ISBN 9780814627242

HOW CAN I [RESIST]

EVIL?

INTRODUCTION (Romans 12:21)

- Reality of spiritual warfare
- Satan = Fallen angel?
  - (Isaiah 14; Luke 10:17–20)
- Old Testament:
  - (Job 1; 1 Chronicles 21:1)
- New Testament:
  - a personal, spiritual being who is in active rebellion against God and has the leadership of many demons like himself
  - (Ephesians 6:11, 12)
- Not to be underestimated
  - cunning
  - evil
  - powerful

1. WHY SHOULD WE BELIEVE THAT THE DEVIL EXISTS?

1. Biblical (Scripture)

- Old Testament
- Jesus
- Peter (1 Peter 5:8–11)
- Paul (Ephesians 6:11, 12)

2. Christians down through the ages (tradition)

- Church fathers
- Reformers
- Ordinary Christians

3. Makes sense of the world (reason)

Mistaken views:

- Disbelief
- Unhealthy interest (Deuteronomy 18:10)

2. WHAT ARE THE DEVIL'S TACTICS? (Genesis 3)

1. Aims to destroy

- (John 10:10)

2. Blinds people

- (2 Corinthians 4:4)

3. Doubt

- (Genesis 3:1)
- (Matthew 4:3, 6)

4. Temptation (Genesis 2:16–17)

- Permission, prohibition, penalty
- Consequences of breaking trust (Genesis 3):
- Shame/embarrassment (v.7)
  – God called them back (vv.9-13)
- Friendship with God broken
  – "they hid" (v.8)
  – "afraid" (v.10)
- They blamed each other (vv.11–13)

5. Accusation

- Accuses God
- Accuses Christians before God (Revelation 12:10)

3. WHAT IS OUR POSITION? (Colossians 1:13)

- Satan defeated on the cross (Colossians 2:15)
- Jesus' disciples given authority over demons (Luke 10:17–20)

4. HOW DO WE DEFEND OURSELVES? [Ephesians 6]

"Put on the full armor of God so that you can take your stand against the devil's schemes" (Ephesians 6:11)

SIX PRACTICAL TIPS:

Keep your relationships right –
breastplate of righteousness [v.14]
- The righteousness of Christ given to us (Philippians 3:9)
- To protect the heart against guilt and condemnation

Focus on Jesus – belt of truth [vv.13–14]
- A grounding in Christian doctrine/truth to counter Satan's lies (John 8:32)

Get involved in service –
boots of the gospel of peace [v.15]
- The readiness to speak of Christ
(Isaiah 52:7–10)

4

Keep trusting God in difficult times –
shield of faith [v.16]

• The opposite of cynicism and scepticism

6

Know your Bible – sword of the Spirit [v.17]
• The word of God
• The only offensive piece of armor
[Hebrews 4.12]

5

Win the battle of the mind –
helmet of salvation [v.17]
• Past, present, future
• To protect the mind against doubt
and accusation

5. HOW DO WE ATTACK?

"The whole world is under the control of the evil one" (1 John 5:19)

The kingdom of God advances through:

1. Prayer (Ephesians 6:18)

- "The weapons we fight with are not the weapons of the world. On the contrary, they have divine power to demolish strongholds" (2 Corinthians 10:4)

2. Action (Luke 7:22)
- Preaching the gospel
- Casting out demons
- Healing the sick, etc.

CONCLUSION

- Evil does exist but we don't need to be afraid
- Defeat evil with prayer and action through the power of the Holy Spirit

Recommended reading
The Screwtape Letters
C. S. Lewis
Zondervan
ISBN 9780060652937

WHY AND HOW

SHOULD I TELL OTHERS?

INTRODUCTION

- Great commission (Matthew 28:16–20)
- Needs of others
- Gospel = good news (about Jesus)
- Two opposite dangers:
  – insensitivity
  – fear
- Key = it arises out of a relationship
- Co-operation with Spirit of God

1. PRESENCE [Matthew 5:13–16]

- We are called to be salt and light (vv.13–14)
- When people know we are Christians, they watch our lives (v.16), i.e., spouses

". . . if any of them do not believe the word, they may be won over without words by the behavior of their wives, when they see the purity and reverence of your lives" (1 Peter 3:1, 2)

2. PERSUASION

"Since . . . we know what it is to fear the Lord, we try to persuade people" (2 Corinthians 5:11; Acts 17:2–4)

- Work out the answers to common questions (1 Peter 3:15)
  – i.e.: "What about other religions?"
  "How can a God of love allow suffering?"

3. PROCLAMATION (John 1:39–46)

- "Come . . . and you will see"
  - we are not all called to be "evangelists" but we are all called to be "witnesses" (v.41)
- Explain ourselves
  - (see appendix at end of chapter)

4. POWER (1 Thessalonians 1:5)

- God's power at work in our lives (1 Corinthians 2:1–5)

5. PRAYER

- For them—to open blind eyes (2 Corinthians 4:4)
- For ourselves—to have boldness (Acts 4:29–31)
- For others (Romans 10:1)

CONCLUSION

- Don't give up (Mark 4:15–20)

Recommended reading

Searching Issues
Nicky Gumbel
Alpha North America
105023

The Case Against Christ
John Young
Hodder & Stoughton
ISBN 9780340908822

APPENDIX

Preparing your testimony

Suggestions:

- Make it short, aim for three minutes—people switch off after that
- Make it personal—don't preach
  - use "I" or "we"—not "you"
- Keep Christ central—they need to follow Him, not you!
- Format
  - a little of your former life
  - how you came into your relationship with Christ
  - something of what it has meant since then
- Write it out in full—it's easier to see the unnecessary words when they're down on paper!

INTRODUCTION

- Introduction of healing to this church
- Our own experience

1. HEALING IN THE BIBLE

1. Old Testament

- Promises of God (i.e.: Exodus 23:25, 26; Psalm 41:3)
- The character of God
  - "I am the Lord who heals you" (Exodus 15:26)
- Examples of God healing (2 Kings 5; Isaiah 38, 39)

2. The ministry of Jesus

- His teaching
  - the kingdom of God (Mark 1:15)
  - proclaimed and demonstrated
- His healings
  - 25% of the Gospels (Matthew 4:23)

- His commissions
  - commission of the Twelve (Matthew 9:35–10:8; Luke 9:1)
  - commission of the seventy-two (Luke 10:1–20)
  - commission of the disciples (Matthew 28:16–20; Mark 16:15–20; John 14:9–14—especially v.12)

2. HEALING IN CHURCH HISTORY

Many examples of healing and miracles (Acts 3:1–10; Acts 5:12–16)

- Early church history
  - i.e.: Irenaeus (140–203)
        Origen (c.185–254)
        Augustine (354–430)

3. HEALING TODAY

- Simplicity
- Love (Matthew 9:36; Mark 1:41)
- Words of knowledge
  - pictures
  - sympathy pain
  - impressions
  - hear or see words
  - words formed on tongue
- Prayer
  - where does it hurt?
  - why does the person
    have this condition?
  - how do I pray?
  - how are they doing?
  - what next?

CONCLUSION

- Persevere
- Keep asking for healing
  through prayer

Recommended reading
Dancer Off Her Feet
Julie Sheldon
Hodder & Stoughton
ISBN 9780340861585

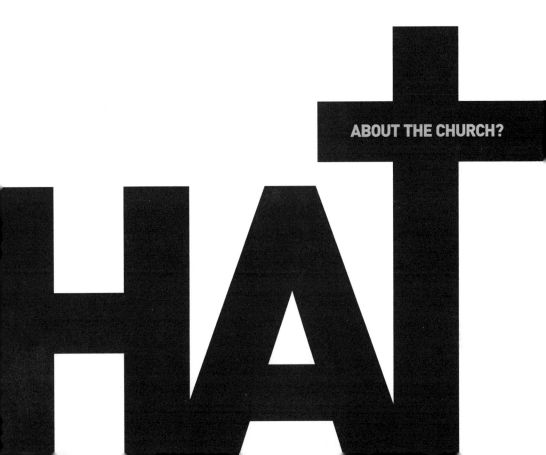

ABOUT THE CHURCH?

HA†

INTRODUCTION

- Popular misconceptions:
  - church = services
  - church = clergy
  - church = a particular denomination
  - church = the building

WHAT IS THE CHURCH?

1. THE PEOPLE OF GOD (1 Peter 2:9, 10)

- Greek word "ekklesia" = an assembly or gathering of people
- Church/kingdom
- Baptism is the visible mark of being a member of the church

Baptism signifies:

- Cleansing from sin (1 Corinthians 6:11)
- Incorporation into Christ's death and resurrection
  (Romans 6:3–5; Colossians 2:12)
- Sealing of the Spirit (1 Corinthians 12:13)

1. Universal church
(Ephesians 3:10, 21; 5:23, 25)

- 1,900 million Christians in the world today
  - persecuted church
  - third world
  - free world

2. **Local churches**

"Galatian churches" (1 Corinthians 16:1)

"The churches in the province of Asia"
(1 Corinthians 16:19)

"All the churches of Christ"

- Cell
  - small group (4–12 people)
  - close friends
  - keynotes
  - confidentiality
  - intimacy
  - accountability (1 John 4:19)
- Congregation
  - pastoral group: 12–50
  - small enough to know others
    and to be known
  - ministry to each other (Ephesians 4:12)
  - exercise of gifts of the Spirit
    (1 Corinthians 12:7–11)
  - open group

- Celebration services
  - festive occasions
    (Passover, Pentecost, New Year)
  - sense of God's greatness
  - weakness: difficult to make friends

2. THE FAMILY OF GOD
(Ephesians 2:14–18) (1 John 5:1)

- **Brothers and sisters to each other**
  (1 John 4:19–5:1)
- **God as our Father** (John 1:12)
- **Importance of unity**
- **Jesus prayed ". . . that they may be
  one"** (John 17:11)
- **"Make every effort to keep the unity
  of the Spirit"** (Ephesians 4:3)

"On the necessary points, unity;
on the questionable points, liberty;
in everything, love"
(Rupertus Meldenius)

- **Faithfulness** (Galatians 6:10)

- **Forgiveness** (Matthew 18:15, 35)
  (Matthew 5:23, 24)
- **Fellowship** (Acts 2:42–47)
  - fellowship with God—Father, Son, and Holy Spirit (1 John 1:3; 2 Corinthians 13:14)
  - and with one another (1 John 1:7; Hebrews 10:24, 25)

3. THE BODY OF CHRIST
(1 Corinthians 12:1–27)

"Saul, Saul, why do you persecute me?" (Acts 9:4)

- **Unity** (Ephesians 4:3–6)
  - "the unity of the Spirit"
- **Diversity** (vv.7–11)
  - "to each one of us grace has been given"
- **Mutual dependence** (vv.14–26)
  - "builds itself up in love, as each part does its work"

4. A HOLY TEMPLE (Ephesians 2:19–22)

- **Built on foundation of apostles and prophets** (v.20)
- **New Testament**
- **Jesus as the cornerstone** (v.20)
- **Indwelt by God's Spirit** (v.21) "a holy Temple"

5. THE BRIDE OF CHRIST
(Ephesians 5:25–27, 32)

- **Christ's love for His church** (v.25)
- **Christ's purpose for His church** (v.27)
  (Revelation 21:2)
- **Our response** (1 Peter 2:9)
  - holiness
  - worship
  - witness

LESSLIE NEWBIGIN WROTE:

"THE CHURCH IS AN HISTORIC REALITY...

beginning with God's call to Abraham and continuing through the ministry of prophets and apostles right down the ages until now. And whether or not the church is popular, big or small, is relatively unimportant. The fact of this great rock, this anvil upon which so many hammers have been worn out, this given reality, needs to be at the centre of our thinking as Christians."

CONCLUSION

- You cannot be a Christian alone
  - get involved in community
- The church is the family of God
  - we are all one family

Recommended reading
I Believe in the Church
David Watson
Hodder & Stoughton
ISBN 9780340372777

HOW
CAN I
MAKE
THE
MOST
OF
THE
REST
OF MY

FE (Romans 12:1-21)

?

1. WHAT SHOULD WE DO?

1. Break with the past

- "Do not conform any longer to the pattern of this world" (v.2)
- "Do not let the world around you squeeze you into its mold" (v.2 J. B. Phillips)

2. Make a new start

- "Let God transform you inwardly by a complete change" (NEB)
  - sincere love (v.9)
  - enthusiasm for the Lord (v.11)
  - harmonious relationships (vv.9–21)

2. HOW DO WE DO IT?

- "Present your bodies . . ."
  Act of will
  - ears
  - eyes
  - mouths
  - hands
  - sexuality
  - time
  - ambitions (Matthew 6:33)
  - money
- ". . . as living sacrifices"
  - it will involve sacrifice
  - it may involve suffering

3. WHY SHOULD WE DO IT?

- What God has planned for our future
  - "his good, pleasing and perfect will" (v.2)
- What God has done for us
  - "in view of God's mercy"

CONCLUSION

- Leave the past behind
  - Jesus offers us a new start
- Sacrifice
  - Jesus made the ultimate sacrifice
  - following Him may involve suffering, but God is with us
  - we can trust God with our future

Recommended reading
Challenging Lifestyle
Nicky Gumbel
Alpha North America
25320

Life in Christ
Raniero Cantalamessa
The Liturgical Press
ISBN 9780814627990

A STEP OF FAITH

Excerpted from *Why Jesus?* by Nicky Gumbel

What Do We Have to Do?

The New Testament makes it clear that we have to do something to accept the gift that God offers. This is an act of faith. The disciple John writes, "God so loved the world that he gave his one and only Son, that whoever believes in him shall not perish but have eternal life" (John 3:16).

Believing involves an act of faith, based on all that we know about Jesus. It is not blind faith. It is putting our trust in a Person. In some ways it is like the step of faith taken by a bride and a bridegroom when they say "I will" on their wedding day.

The way people take this step of faith varies enormously, but I want to describe one way in which you can take this step of faith right now. It can be summarized by three very simple words:

"Sorry"

You have to ask God to forgive you for all the things you have done wrong and turn from everything that you know is wrong in your life. This is what the Bible means by "repentance."

"Thank You"

You believe that Jesus died for you on the cross. You need to thank Him for dying for you and for the offer of His free gifts of forgiveness, freedom, and His Spirit.

"Please"

God never forces His way into our lives. You need to accept His gift and invite Him to come and live within you by His Spirit.

If you would like to have a relationship with God and you are ready to say these three things, then here is a very simple prayer you can pray that will be the start of that relationship:

Lord Jesus Christ,

I am sorry for the things I have done wrong in my life.

(Take a few moments to ask His forgiveness for anything particular that is on your conscience.)

Please forgive me. I now turn from everything that I know is wrong.

Thank You that You died on the cross for me so that I could be forgiven and set free.

Thank You that You offer me forgiveness and the gift of Your Spirit. I now receive that gift.

Please come into my life by Your Holy Spirit, to be with me forever.

Thank you, Lord Jesus. Amen.

Why Jesus? (20072)   A booklet given to all participants at the start of the Alpha course. "The clearest, best illustrated and most challenging short presentation of Jesus that I know." – Michael Green

Why Christmas? (20081)   The Christmas version of *Why Jesus?*

Alpha—Questions of Life (105022)   The Alpha course in book form. In fifteen compelling chapters Nicky Gumbel points the way to an authentic Christianity which is exciting and relevant to the world today.

Searching Issues (105023)   The seven issues most often raised by participants on the Alpha course: suffering, other religions, sex before marriage, the New Age, homosexuality, science and Christianity, and the Trinity.

A Life Worth Living (105024)   What happens after Alpha? Based on the book of Philippians, this is an invaluable next step for those who have just completed the Alpha course, and for anyone eager to put their faith on a firm biblical footing.

How to Run the Alpha Course: Telling Others (16620)   The theological principles and the practical details of how courses are run. Each alternate chapter consists of a testimony of someone whose life has been changed by God through an Alpha course.

Challenging Lifestyle (25320)   Studies in the Sermon on the Mount showing how Jesus' teaching flies in the face of modern lifestyle and presents us with a radical alternative.

30 Days (54057)   Nicky Gumbel selects thirty passages from the Old and New Testament which can be read over thirty days. It is designed for those on an Alpha course and others who are interested in beginning to explore the Bible.

The Heart of Revival (52884)   Ten Bible studies based on the book of Isaiah, drawing out important truths for today by interpreting some of the teaching of the Old Testament prophet Isaiah. The book seeks to understand what revival might mean and how we can prepare to be part of it.

All titles are by Nicky Gumbel, who is the Vicar of
Holy Trinity Brompton in London

We hope you found this course to be both challenging and enriching. If you would like more information about Alpha, please contact the following.

Alpha U.S.A.
2275 Half Day Road
Suite 185
Deerfield, IL 60015
Tel: 800.362.5742
Tel: + 212.406.5269
e-mail: info@alphausa.org
www.alphausa.org

Alpha in the Caribbean
Holy Trinity Brompton
Brompton Road
London SW7 1JA UK
Tel: +44 (0) 845.644.7544
e-mail: americas@alpha.org
www.alpha.org

Alpha Canada
Suite #230 – 11331 Coppersmith Way
Riverside Business Park
Richmond, BC V7A 5J9
Tel: 800.743.0899
Fax: 604.271.6124
e-mail: office@alphacanada.org
www.alphacanada.org

To purchase resources in Canada:

David C. Cook Distribution Canada
P.O. Box 98, 55 Woodslee Avenue
Paris, ON N3L 3E5
Tel: 800.263.2664
Fax: 800.461.8575
e-mail: custserve@davidccook.ca
www.davidccook.ca

It is helpful and encouraging for us to know how this course and the materials we provide are impacting people's lives.

Please tell us your story.

Visit our website—www.alpha.org. Click on the "Share your Story" link.

After completing the form, click "Submit," and we will gladly send you a gift as a thank-you for your time.

If you would like to read the latest news on other Alpha courses, visit our website and click on the sign up for Alpha News link.

Thank you!